HISTORY IS
YOUR OWN HEARTBEAT

*History Is
Your Own Heartbeat*

POEMS BY

Michael S. Harper

UNIVERSITY OF ILLINOIS PRESS
Urbana, Chicago, London

© 1971 by Michael S. Harper

Manufactured in the United States of America

Library of Congress Catalog Card No. 74-139806

Paper: 252 00145 1

Cloth: 252 00144 3

Acknowledgment is made to the following publications in which some of these poems first appeared: *The Black Scholar* ("High Modes"); *For Gwen, with Love* ("Madimba: Gwendolyn Brooks"); *The Massachusetts Review* ("The Morse Recount: History as Bridge, A Convention," "Time for Tyner: Folksong," "Mission: 1 January 70"); *Field* ("Ruth's Blues"); *Black Swamp Review* ("The Dance of the Elephants"); *Kayak* ("The Faculty Club, Portland, Oregon").

FOR SHIRL
who loves trees
more than water,
and me more than them

PART ONE

Ruth's Blues

FOR RUTH MCLAUGHLIN BUFFINGTON

BLUE RUTH: AMERICA

I am telling you this:
the tubes in your nose,
in the esophagus,
in the stomach;
the small balloon
attached to its end
is your bleeding gullet;
yellow in the canned
sunshine of gauze,
stitching, bedsores,
each tactoe cut
sewn back
is America:
I am telling you this:
history is your own heartbeat.

Married to rural goldmines
in southern Minnesota,
your money is land, horses,
cows all of metal:
the area is German;
the religion Gothic, acute,
permanent, in white heat
and telephone wires;
you live with a family where
each issue is food,
where word is appetite
you hunger in: hunting
your slough for teal;
beating your sons with machinery
and your oiled might;
setting your chickens to peck
your children; roping them homegrown
to the tractors and cockleburs,
giving them no private thoughts
but rebellion:

fish and hunt for surplus
acreage to corncrib you up,
lutheran or catholic
in taste and ambition;
love grandchildren,
love potatoes,
love beans, love venison,
love pheasant, love berries,
love bass, love rocks
become fossils, love sweetcorn,
shucked in guts, silently
burrowing what grows
but can't love, burgeoning,
lovely, like this.

The windows of America
are faceless, incestuous screens
pumiced in pure glass,
triangular, innocent,
wired white hoods
cropped in green grass.

Comatose and armed
explorers brought salt water
from the ocean to boil
in three kettles as an offering;

The Indians smoked
on the mountaintrails
in buck heat
high along the Columbia;

Lewis and Clark,
their slave, York,
took their salt up
in their webbings;

the meat now cured,
the lumber stink off
the river,
fertilize no soil
without Indian blood
or red roses.

"Stirrups, leggings, a stainless
steel slide, a dishpan, sheet,
a thread spool, scissors,
three facemasks, smocks, paper
overshoes, a two-way mirror, dials:"
the head and left arm
cruise out, almost together,
and you drop into gloves,
your own ointment
pulling your legs
binding your cord; the cheesed
surface skin, your dark
hairless complexion, the metallic room,
orchestrate and blow up your lungs,
clogged on protein and vitamins,
for the sterile whine of the delivery
room and your staff of attendants.
It is free exercise when the cord's
cut; you weigh in for the clean up
as your mother gets her local
for her stitches: boy, 6′ 13″.

As you breathe easily, your mother's
mother is tubed and strapped,
hemorrhaging slowly from her varices;
your two dead brothers who could
not breathe are berries
gone to rot at our table:
what is birth but death
with complexity: blood, veins,
machinery and love: our names.

GOOD SAMARITAN HOSPITAL

"Point It out, Point It out to Me"

The story goes: wide purple
eyes woven in sugar, we add
some vinegar and hot dye;
the non-toxic drip of our
continent on inhabitants
is odorless as lightning;
we hug the tributaries
to our skin of tobacco—
the cotton crop perfectly dry;
the drink is cane sugar
which yeasts on the docks,
the blue-black molasses
shucked and popped in the oven.

The best trained cooks
are the best trained spies
who shift the vats where the lab
learns more about blood sugar
and hemoglobin—
black and white ice cream
bins pucker this sexual
imagery; the rarest blood
rose is skinned by white hands;
a garden is a white woman
with a penchant for tropical flowers.
What is the smell of black semen
stuck in white wombs
in 1876 when the troops withdraw?

We explore the illiterate halls
with a photographic eye;
the flick we've made is our bible
for which there's no cost;
we splice in our parts,
"The Birth of a Nation,"
a wide angle close-up,
buck, posse, a good horse.

LOVELY'S DAUGHTERS: VISITORS

We packed our cuts
and insect bites with rich damp earth.

The breeze swung our own birches
in clots of music.

We ate the tangled punch grapes,
crushed brown bodies in vines.

4-inch nails snagged our blankets,
gowned on the treehouse stair,

bats flew, tangling our hair;
we danced with the spider crayfish.

Naked, on the hot night road,
we squashed fireflies on our chests
as they burned;

fallen corn, haymow, cuckleburs,
the unplowed rocks, hail,
swollen tornadoes cracking

our bedwater;
these centigrade nights
we cuddle our stink to keep warm.

The bees circling,
blood down our legs,
we stuffed soybean leaves in us.

Now we swell in the visitor cove
in the fifth floor scissor-light,
punctured bells on a rope
twenty feet from your door,
six portwind odors
staved in the toxic night;
your grandchildren grow
taut as sandpaper in your
pregnant daughters—one
in serape, one in wood shoes—
we switch the wheelchair
between us, witnesses sworn
under oath, music our own heartbeats,
digging our poetry with our nails.

The tubes in my nostrils
occasionally itch;
an off-red bulbed balloon
sits inflated on my stomach
in the esophagus;
I have not bled near the bulb
since Sunday; their inlets
of apparatus; the goggles of white
shimmering eggs, evening moss,
the haze of abortion, after birth
to let history die.

My surgical nurse has dug
her twins in caesarian section,
black boy and girl, one month
premature: morphine hums
these weatherclocks, cleaning fluid
mopping one cry; the boy dies
on an adjacent stretcher,
the girl lies there but will not
stop breathing; one in a newspaper,
the other a blanket discovered
outside to be cleaned in the nursery:
an eight-hour shift is a family line.

I swim in the southwest
corner of the freight elevator,
an annulled, murderous witness
switching cots over two water-bagged floors.

CLAN MEETING: BIRTHS AND NATIONS:
A BLOOD SONG

We reconstruct lives in the intensive
care unit, pieced together in a buffet
dinner: two widows with cancerous breasts
in their balled hands; a 30-year-old man
in a three-month coma
from a Buick and a brick wall;
a woman who bleeds off and on from her gullet;
a prominent socialite, our own nurse,
shrieking for twins, "her bump gone";
the gallery of veterans, succored,
awake, without valves, some lungs gone.

Splicing the meats with fluids
seasoned on the dressing room
table, she sings "the bump gone"
refrain in this 69-degree oven,
unstuffing her twin yolks
carved from the breast, the dark meat
wrapped in tinfoil and clean newspaper;
the half black registered nurse
hums her six years in an orphanage,
her adopted white family,
breaded and primed in a posse,
rising in clan for their dinner.

We reload our brains as the cameras,
the film overexposed
in the x-ray light,
locked with our double door
light meters: race and sex
spooled and rung in a hobby;
we take our bundle and go home.

13

WITCH WINGS AND SKILLED HANDS:
THE NURSE'S SONG

This man is black;
this man is white;
this skin is made up
for third-degree burns.

Lennie is painted in;
why is a black man
father of this child;
what is his name?

We lay in blankets
on storage 2x4's
with the nails removed,
beneath us, inflatable mats:

I have these pills;
I can fly to Seattle;
I can marry;
I can give up children;

above my breasts a mobile,
a dripping nosebleed, the blood
smearing his hairless
chest, painting a crack.

Two eggs slip on the bannered walls,
their yolks blurred like flypaper;
the uterus swells in a flowering nest
while the venous twins thicken.

This spotted discharge creamery,
diet and exercise, whips numb legs
"up five flights of stairs":
auburn curls, corsetted, loose gowned.

My children rise up as vapor,
dice on our picnic table;
the matching eyes hum in brown froth,
rhythmic and open as a hang-band.

The yeasty bump rises with the full moon.
White, eight months pregnant,
in the Portland ghetto,
fetters, and a uniform, all black.

"Ungie, Hi Ungie"

A two-year-old boy
is a blossom in the intensive
care aisle, small as
a ball-bearing,
round, open and smooth;
for a month, in his first
premature hours, his shaved
head made him a mohawk Indian
child, tubes the herbs
for his nest, a collapsed lung
the bulbous wing of a hawk.
Slivered into each sole
in an intravenous solution
to balance his losses
or what they take out
for the lab; the blue spot
on his spine is a birth
mark of needle readings;

the hardened thighs immune
from 70 shots of various
drugs of uneven depth; the chest
is thick with congestion: bad
air and mucus—good air and pure
oxygen; jerky pouch buffalo lungs—
It does not surprise me
when he waits patiently for his
grandmother, over her five-hour
painless operation; he has
waited in his isolette
before: the glow in his eyes
is for himself, will and love:
an exclamation of your name:
"*Ungie, hi Ungie*"; you are saved.

One's still in, a goose egg's
made its own bile duct;
the 120 wound pearls
season before doctors,
diamonds to be sorted,
etched in pancreas juice;
they photograph this collection
of off-color radishes,
milky and boiled,
for the medical museum.

A gallstone's seed is berry
wild in fuzz, boned
and filleted, cured,
for each special attack.

So many transfusions
have seeded in sediment
the antibodies won't be identified;
a pint of O blood,
pickles from the lab,
a miraculous find;
they pick the unetherized
weedbeds of tissue and stone
for leaks or obstructions;
cut you like mush melon
suckled in worms
picking your liver
and gall bladder
the color of squash.

Jaundice was your tenth
year on the farm;
five conscious hours
they pickax inside;
you float down this aisle
boxed, fingered, eyed.

ECHOES FROM SWING SHIFT:
DOCTOR, DOCTOR IS A MISSIONARY

The head nurse has whiplash;
her eyes, her ovaries
salute you in the appointment
center; your doctor is fixated,
updating his knowledge, the Congo,
and of you: green humus
clothing, x-rays and crusts of bread;
doctor, doctor is a missionary.
In Africa, an open-heart surgeon,
and on your operating table,
his prayers lead his hands
into the marble collection,
the lost gall bladder,
horizontal sutures and your heartbeat
beating the herniated count
of three, as a limerick,
or a chant:
"She's getting awfully
low"; "No I'm not."
The artist in you spins
out a rhyme about cherry,
cherry pie, the price
of your operations;
cherry, cherry pie, without seeds.

THE BROADWAY BRIDGE:
EXITS AND VISITS

We race across this fecal
bridge four times a day
full of exits and homemade
wheatgerm oil, soya flour,
six pairs of tracks,
truckers crinking their necks
for the perfect wingshot.
We move on the elevators
to the odor of cabbage,
wheelchair tracks, walking
crutches with white hair;
with our bible-belt appetites
fishing us in, we hook our arms
to an ox-cart of images,
orchards of fibrous black hair,
a puffy, soiled, diapered complexion;
we drink bedwater for flowers.
On our way home, a pocked
drunk seaman drapes his clothes
on the railing to swing out
for the somersault into the Willamette;
a barge swoops by without motors;
he crawls aboard by arrangement.
The following day his clothes are still
there, weeded and patched and clean;
but for a single goose egg
which might move, you map out
the next move to go home.

HISTORY AS BANDAGES:
POLKA DOTS AND MOONBEAMS

One is an igloo
of whalebone and oil
and a poisonous gas;
one is a canoe under water
laden with wild rice,
grubs, and Indian arrows;
one is a banjo
packed with thin dirt
in Richmond, Virginia:
Gabriel: 1800;
one is a round bubble
of mustard rock
broken on an Indian squaw;
one is a print of a buffalo,
bearded, masked, made
musty skinned hair.

The white rectangular
patchwork covers all these
national wounds kept
secretly bound, at night,
absorbing color and blood and bones
of all shapes and disguises.

ONE LIVES, ONE DIES:
BOTH/AND: A CHOICE OF COLORS

Wild rice grows along the banks
of your house, stilted
and holding you up;
your gowned daughters squeeze
pimples and curls and magpie
around the kitchen, ironing
and rinsing their mouths—
bass after minnows and frogs;
you think of the twin-grained
children in the intensive care
unit, and their parents,
race-hate, musical machines
that tear at your stitches,
the leadfilling gas from the trucks,
butchers in green smocks
and your own life in the wick
of Christmas pine and pheasants:
almost completely gutted, you count
your three mixed fledglings:
Roland, Stephen, Patrice;
seed, pollen, pine.

24TH AVENUE: CITY OF ROSES: ANESTHESIA: 2

You sit, puckered and dry,
on a wicker chair on our porch;
the roses and oaks enclose you in
mists of blossoms and garden
vegetables in your own yard;
sloughs of children are mallards,
your grandson a black and tan goose
with no neck and loose hair,
a pugged bill, unafraid,
who has pulled you back
from death with his own
voice: *"hi Ungie, Hi."*

I think of the phosphates
that gurgle in the drains
of your eyes, the salts
and vitamins, a stacked deck
on a seven-foot shelf,
baked dishes burnished in tubes
of fine print
surrounding the breakfast nook;

sometimes sulphur won't mix
with you thin blood,
you yellow into a spacious bug,
bloom for six hours, nap
or sew or read nursery-
song patter to sprout at our table.
Yellow again as your liver
shrinks to normal size,
nocturnal buds fusing to rend,
your eyes jelly and slim
in the evening porchlight,
go out in sudden pain,
rekindle, electric as smoke;
we fire our thermostat
measuring your meal and toilet.

TWEEDLE ON TWEEDLE:
RUTH'S LAST CHILD

She leaps on branches
in moccasined feet
with the agility of ice
breaking up in spring thaw;
as the night bulb
frostbite eats her legs
she walks from farmhouse
to farmhouse in kneesox
and ballerina shorts
as the snow grows
after the winter dance.
Planes hawk pass,
southern valley,
and the blue ice
for prints her body
made, choked on field grass,
chewing the cobs, unbucking
the pronged teeth
bored to a paste,
squinting after scratches.

Now she's escaped
death by freezing,
her son backpacked
in diapers and a hat,
small hump with antlers
in the brush,
a birdling with warble
like a thrush;
they disappear on a trolley
going west,
sparkled by the Minnesota
woods, criss-crossed
in their homemade cotton hoods,
airy, bobbing, in a rush.

VITAMIN K: DON'T BLEED ON ME

This clots the blood in throat
cancer, a cut-fingered blister
through the neck, a keyhole
of calloused knuckle, a hinge.
We carry it in lungs of glass,
tinted with pastel labels,
sold, outright, as pink
aspirin and fertilizer;
the residue is left for you
bleeders who ache at terror
in your own blood, and in others,
sloughed in gardens and gravesites.

We made an unnatural community
in a thicket
a half mile from the road,
near New London;
fed from our freezer stock full
of rhubarb, moose and corn;
fought the long winter
with snowshoes and ice fishing,
sunflowers, operas
to blow the snow;
the letters that sat at
the roadside frosted with news.

To avoid each other
we sat long hours over coffee
plotting the last thirty years
and our failure, organized
farmers too stubborn to yield;
we spoke of dead relatives
our own age, and their parents
still burying their children
as ours hung on to our gowns;
building our fences and boats,
our lake garden,
the planned year a new home
clotting our blood and our soil.

RELAPSE: LONG LAKE, MINNESOTA:
SPIRIT AS WONDER

Blood from the varices,
the stool black
as sunburnt wire
threading a portal
bypass retrenching
this blood, *Ruth,*
drawn and quartered
outside, these eyesacks
having seen all fly
in a spiral after dark.

Fireflies sputter
on the face of this lakesite
named for the Indians,
our blood, Kandiyohi;
our hearts arrest,
congealed into black flags
of pigment and plastic;
your grandsons climb,
vines in your firefly eyes.

All your own blood gone,
gallstones and bladder,
the varicose veins whose splinters
are nuclear bones,
white black lake ice
and our rotting docks.

Snowmobiles die,
the oaks belch green,
these grey skies break
long sphinctered handles,
your light kindles, eye dots
in the banked snow;

clots of homemade clouds
blacken as your yeasty
blood goes to its hearth
of plastic circuitry—
loved 'til you die
all at once, deer, raccoon,
garden-goose, *Ruth,*
prancing on her wiry wheels:
wondrously fixed at her dancing,
we wait for her last cry.

Soul and race
are private dominions,
memories and modal
songs, a tenor blossoming,
which would paint suffering
a clear color but is not in
this Victorian house
without oil in zero degree
weather and a forty-mile-an-hour wind;
it is all a well-knit family:
a love supreme.
Oak leaves pile up on walkway
and steps, catholic as apples
in a special mist of clear white
children who love my children.
I play "Alabama"
on a warped record player
skipping the scratches
on your faces over the fibrous
conical hairs of plastic
under the wooden floors.

Dreaming on a train from New York
to Philly, you hand out six
notes which become an anthem
to our memories of you:
oak, birch, maple,
apple, cocoa, rubber.
For this reason Martin is dead;
for this reason Malcolm is dead;
for this reason Coltrane is dead;
in the eyes of my first son are the browns
of these men and their music.

PART TWO

History as Personality

If you had a choice of colors
which one would you choose my brothers
if there was no day or night,
which would you prefer to be right?

from "Choice of Colors"
by THE IMPRESSIONS

MARTIN'S BLUES

He came apart in the open,
the slow motion cameras
falling quickly
neither alive nor kicking;
stone blind dead
on the balcony
that old melody
etched his black lips
in a pruned echo:
*We shall overcome
some day—*
Yes we did!
Yes we did!

MADIMBA: GWENDOLYN BROOKS

Music is its own heartbeat

Double-conscious sister in the veil,
Double-conscious sister in the veil;
Double-conscious sister in the veil:
Double-conscious sister in the veil.

You beat out the pulse with your mallets,
the brown wishbone anemones
unflowered and unworn in Chicago congo
prints, images, otherness, images

from the fossilbank: Madimba.
Black Man; I'm a black man; black—
A-um-ni-pad-me-hum—
another brother gone:

"the first act of liberation
is to destroy one's cage"—
a love supreme;
a love supreme.

Images: words: language
typing the round forms: Juneteenth,
baby, we free, free at last:
black man, I'm a black man.

A garden is a manmade vision,
rectangular, weeded, shelled,
pathed, hosed, packed in,
covered with manure, pruned;

I own you; you're mine, you
mine, baby: to bear unborn things.
Double-conscious sister in the veil:
Double-conscious sister in the veil.

Black woman: America is artful
outside time, ideal outside space;
you its only machine: Madimba:
Double-conscious sister in the veil.

ORAL LIGHT: URBANA, ILLINOIS

Beacons: the cat teeth
refracting boycotted angles
of personality, here;
the shoeless professors
shuck the cat paw
silence in academy bins,
human manure traced to the waterhole.
They reach their cane poles out
for catfish in sun-glassed
pools of catfood;
but there's no bite,
the pull beneath water
snapping lines—worms
and delicate sinkers—
or the wind changes,
rippling the pale flecks,
phosphorescent, as the leaves turn.

In the catlight dinner air,
tonal and whispered as sauce,
the floured catfish puffs in grease;
they sprinkle their salts
in the candle waxed, oral light.

for John F. Callahan

THE MORSE RECOUNT: HISTORY AS BRIDGE, A CONVENTION

There are thirteen bingo tables,
an arcade of hairsprays floating
in an Oregon barnburning, cameras
taping challengers, recorders,
the droplets of rain which, in dust,
settle like feet on highwires,
bodies cloaked to attention,
fingered into poses of mourning:
war, hunger, ghettocong, drugs,
the congressional mafia.
We count in triplicate,
striking the *no* votes as ushers
at the world series, nothing at stake
but our buttons, callousing
our high-tension feet, the game
lost, the urge to piss
on our cards on the auction table.

The process of government is ritual:
darts, blowgun, a soup pot,
twigs, herbs, warriors in ascending
order, the poisonous meat;
beginning to eat we nourish
our cooked lottery
with blood sacrifice
on our counting table.

for John F. Callahan

41

JAZZ STATION

Some great musicians got no place to play

Above the freeway, over the music,
we speak of the strategy of poems,
bleeding wives who ulcerate
our voices rhythming in the cut-heat
Portland stink from the Willamette River;
arteries of smog fixate this place
in each recording, music, music, on *Impulse.*
This little racist community has few friends;
thousands of deerslayers hum into Beaverton,
the one talk show driven out for their talk
as the liberals dig in to KGO out of San Francisco;
we troop toward the Lloyd Center for the ice-skating,
the colorette bloomered dream merchants on rented skates,
and the *Sunday Chronicle* near the big hotel.

The poets, man and wife, write in the dimming air,
their daughter in the toy rooms connecting them,
the typewriter tacking the nails and snaps of her gown.
This image of separation begins in adoption:
her mother adopted out in San Jose; her father
disowned, abandoned, torn out of the will; her name:
    Phoebe.

And the sun does shine on them for this visit
in squat pigeontoes, and this beach ball sings.

for Sandy and Henry Carlile

PHOTOGRAPHS: A VISION OF MASSACRE

We thought the grass
would grow up quickly
to hide the bodies.
A brother sloped across
his brother, the patched
clay road slipping
into our rainy season
of red, our favorite color.

When the pictures came
we spoke of our love
for guns, oiled and glistening
in the rich blood of machines:
bodies, boys and girls, clutching
their private parts, oiled,
now slightly pink,
and never to be used.

FALL SCENE

Thistles, straight and spined
as unbereted hair,
punch the glass
on the mantel
bruising the light
album covers and photographs
bookended above the shelves.
The fossil quality of weed,
the unhomogenous trail
in the eucalyptus patch,
the briar drinking fountain
over the reservoir,
the plea of my three-
year-old fleabitten son
scratching scabs
on his wet shirtfront,
the bluejay wind
cushioning the lunchbags
in pockets of smoke
eating its bread,
nourishes the enameled blanket.

A neighbor boy
phases the late summer
in, his burning bedroom,
how the firemen
wetted our ceiling
while his grandmother
hacked our door
trying to arouse us.

The blueblack lips,
Crocus Indian children
behind the red porch,
knock the stereolight
to vibration:
weeds left here
burn in the racial fall.

COME BACK BLUES

I count black-lipped
children along river-creek,
skimming between bog,
floating garbage
logs, glistening tipped
twilight and night beaks;
the drowned drown again
while their parents
picket the old library and pool
special fish
taken up in poison—
you've come back
to count bodies again
in your own backyard.

for Robert F. Williams

THE FACULTY CLUB, PORTLAND, OREGON

These are liberals in starched
dungarees the color of sharkskin;
this is a college senior who hunts
seals in the Yukon with a hammer;
this is our president, his testes
in magnified glass, the color of crystal.
Our language is clear, polished,
of cast wax, the breathing measured,
each in his box seat, honed and ready;
academic freedom, black studies;
pup tents on our lawn's meridian,
camped and potted in our orchidean
garden, freshened with incest-manure,
humanities, clean funds from directors
and the government.
The conservatives, the lower division,
always against war, negotiate
our flints, feathered gowns, tenure,
genteel wines, and this song.

for Robert E. Michael

TIME FOR TYNER: FOLKSONG

The medley goes like this:
We sit in a bar in a draft
from the swinging door as
some patrons leave in wings
which are fleecelined coats
echoing with the ice cream
red of the police pick-up van;
an African instrument is not
the piano; an African village
is not the Both/And; an African
waltz is not in 3/4.

It strikes me in his juice
is the love of melody;
he thumbs the solo piano
in a wickerchair blues
tripping a rung tune in its
scratching black keys
shimmering in the plant light:
we are all covered green.

It is a political evening:
posters of Mingus and Trane,
recordings of Bud Powell,
Bird under false names,
the economy of Miles;
I take it in scratchpad
English in the waxed light
as his liner notes pucker
on our lips in this country
abiding and earless.

for McCoy Tyner,
and gone musicians

THE HAYWARD COUNCIL OF CHURCHES:
SPIRIT AS RITUAL:

On Interviewing a New Member Unbeknownst to Them

Ongoing, and ongoing,
and ongoing they come
choosing chambers, choosing their kin
leadening the plastic walls
as spirits relax
germinal in quiet.

What if one insisted on
a dance made equal to their lives?
or made them spirits
in themselves made wise?
or conjured up a number,
gearing lives,
and hooked them to them
in a special guise?

Passion and commitment
temporize:
ongoing, and ongoing,
and ongoing they come;
germination is a quiet dream,
personality its richest ream.

When in answer to their dreams
they ask,
what is it that makes its mask,
answer it is emptiness that runs within,
penitence, unerring sin.

Murder is the academic game
opting in a soporific name;
vision, vision, personality,
make redemptive, manly polity.

for John F. Callahan

THE DANCE OF THE ELEPHANTS

Part I

The trains ran through the eleven
nights it took to vacate the town;
relatives and lovers tacked in a row
on the button-board sidings,
wails of children tossed in a pile
wails of women tossed in a salad
to be eaten with soap and a rinse.
Those who took all they had to the borders,
those who took their bottles
three centuries old, those who
thought only of language, the written
word, are forgiven.
One daughter is riding on the train
above her mother, above her mother,
into the tunnel of the elephants.

Culture tells us most about its animals
singing our children asleep, or let them
slip into a room as smoothly as
refrigeration.

Part II

To be comforted by Swiss music
is a toy elephant in a box,
skimming the nickelplated air.
Beethoven's a passion dance
forgotten in a stamped coin—
it is magic—it is magic—

We dance the old beast round the fireplace,
coal engines fuming in a row,
elephant chimes in a toy rain—
human breath skimming the air.

We skim the air—
it is magic—the engines
smelling the chimes,
Beethoven chiming the magic—
we escape it on a train.

Sung in America,
the song some telescopic sight,
a nickelplated cream,
a small girl cuddles her elephant,
the song in the streets
leaping the train windows,
and what love as the elephant chimes.

from an anecdote
by Susan Kirschner

Weeds are in her face
she skates in 20-below
thin air skipping the risen
pockets of lake ice
moving with urgency
in her dance—
we have swept an icerink
in a circle
and wetted it down
with lake water
from the electric pump
the auger-holes on the beach;
a white goose is the dance
of me, the vatting ice,
the green surface eyes
in the dance, for she seeks
her gone children there,
in this dance;
goose-thin, the nostrils
like stalks, her sons
shimmering in the lake ice,
goose and crescent
perfect, two figurines.

In this decade I expect
the environment to pull
each into place
as weedbanks giving cover
to my goose.
I stroke her open-ended
neck and watch the air.
To watch my goose in dance,
to watch her fly
and with the breakup ice
in spring, to fish
our children back,
to make them sing before her eyes:
then watch my goose, my dance,
her arching neck a crescent
open-ended.

for Shirl

HOUSE ON MIRAMAR, SAN FRANCISCO

Five years in the house
of pisces, the bellbottom
faces of sons
all shining the mantel mirror
and the fireplace
stacked with matches,
weeds, the dead books
curled to unworkable precision;
the western sun bleeds
through the seasonal fog,
the belly of woman
pregnant and puffy
with seeds from African pottery
or the song of Billie Holiday
on a big band of air.

Breeze from the open fireplace,
the wind crookeyes down the flue,
black ashes of newsprint and cartons
milky and burnt: incineration.
What they did to no. 2 and 3 sons:
firebombed from the Kaiser nursery,
the phlegm and algae cut away:
medicinal incineration;
what they did to this young girl
in the late cot sun
is the workbench history of disease.

Dahlias in the yard
the bulbs hammering up
as snails after milky submersion;
flower and weed,
crossbreeded boys sway
on the rusty trapeze
of their mother's hipbones
bent and billowy,
womanous nursery with dugs.

Cherokee skin, Indian
colors, bushes, sanitary
padding, ridges of woman
broken and panting in the sun.

for Shirl

MOVIN' WES

Gone from us
this guitar
where the bull resides
his heat
gone from us,
Movin' Wes rides
his beginnings:

Wes, guitar, Movin' Wes:
Charlie Christian
Movin' Wes
Leadbelly, Movin' Wes
John Lee Hooker
Movin' Wes
B. B. King, Movin' Wes
Wes Montgomery,
Movin' Wes:

Shaped like a heart
this guitar is its own organ;
its gnarled hands
bled octaves
in men's veins,
their children
the stickpin controls:
Movin' Wes:

Gone from us,
electronic ears
tune on
Movin' Wes:

Unrecorded,
Movin' Wes
blew with Trane
"Favorite Things"
so hard, out there,
guitar became man:
Movin' Wes:

Instrument
Favorite Things
all alive:
Movin' Wes:

THE ICE-FISHING HOUSE:
LONG LAKE, MINNESOTA

Checking the traps
on the way out
along the iced beaches
the birches sift,
connecting a groundwork
overcome without woman,
this particular snow.

At the first point
the bunny boots soak
up the foot of water
under snow—
we slip in the single
tracks on thick ice
zigzagging northeast
to the house marked "Schultz."

The three trap doors
prism as we auger down,
sinker, minnow, 28 feet;
the kerosene stove heats
the first croppy bed
and we eat.

This greenhouse is set
on stilts, drawn by snowmobiles
over Thanksgiving;
6 x 8 x 6
compass, sextant, wheel
blue light.

Thirty-five crappies in a pail
go with us as we leave this hut;
jackrabbit tracks
cross to the point.
Bunny boot snowshoes or full
fishpail, these traps remain unfilled.

The hollow sounds in this wind,
Kandiyohi, Indian place-names
I've heard in my grandmother's voice
calling the Chippewa in
calling the Chippewa in

for Howard L. Buffington

BLUES AS PREMATURITY:
RESPIRATORY DISTRESS SYNDROME:
TAKE 2, 3

Green gowned, the hairy
arm works over the tabletop,
magical chants over the boy,
chants between breaths—

He fills the tube with new
air in this premature corridor,
pure crystalized lungs
backed up in protein.

Paradigm, turning,
with his windbags clogged

this son gives out only
as the blood vessels break into chant:

green man, sidekick, father,
give up, give in.

for Reuben, for Michael

AIR CURRENTS: NO SMOKING

These soft darkened pen
marks smoother into pilings,
these crosses measured—
instruments flick out.
Bodies of elliptical water
tremble in grained fingers
as the mountains pass
alive, blown clean
with ferns, blur bushes,
pines, blending green sacks,
as each mountain grows
in the earth.

The air percolates
these short banks
great salt licks
as compass and pen,
weatherblind,
puncture the exposed chest,
each face pulsing:
Bladder moon!
Bladder moon!

ON FINDING OUT THAT MOSES WAS
AN EGYPTIAN

This day have I set before you Life and Death, Good and Evil;
choose ye, therefore, Life and Good.—Old Testament

You survive, dig it?
by yourself.
Any body of water
is a gas to cross—
ten parables in stone—
work out cryptic god.

Had to give it
to a brother.
Who else could understand
that *modal* shit—
a mode reveals its own truth—
huh, baby?

for W. E. B. DuBois

64

PISCES' HOUSE: ERNEST JABALI, MOON RISING

Even as your father's hands collapse
the sutured, paralytic womb
swims to the music, your mother's
pants, the unnatural caressing
chant: Jabali: strong.

Joined in the hands and heads,
the locked chuckle of your palmwine
spirits, ancestors, clear in their
offerings; loved by those
who've blessed you, whole,
the spirits wither and strike
at the beating heart,
breastbone, esophagus,
bloodmilk your mother conjures
up in the songy prose,
afterbirth of nourishment
and remembrance.

Now in the promised cradle
you etch in the images
of your father's fathers,
images, Jabali, paid
in their blood,
their songs open,
caroming, angle to angle,
in the world that is yours.

for John and Sandra Stewart

DEALT, IN THE NAME OF LOVE

"Why shouldn't I go for trying to change things, for trying to deal everybody a brand new deck?"

Dealt; dealt; dealt;
cards won't change suit;
paradigm
court jesters
mimic you
changing clothes:
Jack 'a diamonds,
puttin' on dog,
legal as a tabernacle
and this choir:
"there's a man
goin' 'round
takin' names"—

Dealt; dealt; dealt;
a straight flush,
five of a kind,
black ace on top of spade,
jack and panther
suited up
in a pig's magic:
Sack 'a Woe,
wet dream,
incineration,
penis and a colt .44.

Dealt; dealt; dealt;
suits changing hands,
kitty's a bloodbank,
bloody Mary's
pregnant with song:
queen 'a hearts,
ace 'a spades,
jack 'a diamonds:
what makes your big heads
so hard: *Mop!*

NEWSLETTER FROM MY MOTHER:
8:30 A.M., December 8, '69

"1100 Exposition
4115 South Central
and some place on 55th Street
were all subject to seige
at 5:30 this morning.
The police arrived with search warrants.

"At the present time
1100 Exposition
and the house on 55th Street
have fallen.

"4115 South Central
is still resisting;
they have sandbagged
the place and are wearing
bullet-proof vests,
tear gas masks;

"the whole area is cordonned off,
Wadsworth School is closed;
the police are clearing a hotel
next door to get a better vantage.

"The police deny this is part
  of a nationwide program to wipe
  out the Panther Party;
  one of the fellows here at work,
  who lives in the area,
  says that they were clearing the streets
  last night, arresting people
  on any pretext,
  and that the jails are full.

"(I have to wait until my boss
  starts her class in the conference
  room so I can turn on the radio
  and get the latest news.)

"10 A.M.:
  The Panthers are surrendering
  1 at a time."

                    for Katherine Johnson Harper

THE ANGELS LEVINE

In this ear
a message and a wound;
the sound goes out
each ear becomes the ground.

"Jazz ain't enough anymore, poetry neither"

We watch this mark make time
an image of hair
thumb women making bread
from grain at the backyard.
The fruit trees
hammer his name
in their thumping
and the bush comes out.
What history,
that of drugs,
that of love,
handclasped in a star,
his name.

Levine, Levine,
jazz ain't enough
anymore,
poetry neither;
making the bread
the bread comes out,
thumping army bush,
machine on machine.

Drug Merchant got
your baby,
won't let him go
watch this mark
make time:
learn to count,
Levine, Levine, Levine.

High, high on music on *Impulse,*
we spin jams to the count of three
sons who won't mix
even their shoes
to the same beat.
The indelible needles
cut the scalp
the layers of bone
winking to the pulse
of an eighth Indian
blood near the nerve
center of America:
cut close to memory
all life calcified
with your bones,
they cut in the hearing
for awhile, cut out the bone
you make to ossify the pain.

This way to the bones
of Spain.
Bones calcify
as eyes so blue
they shine in the dark,
colors wrinkle on your face,
you read the lips of those
you love and your man's enemies:
none of this insight,
woven in its gold,
is recorded in the stars.
Pinched out, quarter
notes of the last octave
of hearing, you bless
us all with your song.

"Give me a son with humor,"
he said; the angels
swung into view
from a chin-up
bar, over
this charred grassbed
of the Indian earth;
hot bowls
sat near the fireplace
these cold nights,
or took up their games
when night fell.

Animals came:
pigs, horses,
dogs came;
the war went on,
animals losing their wings,
calls for day
began; one cut loose
machines and habits
that are physical,
psychic America
pulled at its weight
on this chin-up bar,
threads, panels,
money belts,
tearing at these walls
to let angels and animals
through.

for Philip and Frances Levine

DON'T EXPLAIN:

Culture as Science as Language as Cannibal

Herbicides ain't drano;
defoliants ain't aspirin;
pathogenic bacteria ain't crest;
virus ain't contac;
toxins ain't pepto;
napalm ain't vicks:

what dem?
what dey do?

PART THREE

High Modes

Supernigger's dead; long live the mf!
"Music, being an expression of the human
heart, expresses what is happening."

FOR OLIVER LEE JACKSON

I

"BIRD LIVES": CHARLES PARKER
IN ST. LOUIS

Last on legs, last on sax,
last in Indian wars, last on *smack*,
Bird is spacious, *Bird* is alive,
horn, unplayable, before, after,
right now: it's heroin time:
smack, in the melody a trip;
smack, in the Mississippi;
smack, in the drug merchant trap;
smack, in St. Louis, Missouri.

We knew you were through—
trying to get out of town,
unpaid bills, connections
unmet, unwanted, unasked,
Bird's in the last arc
of his own light: *blow Bird!*
And you did—
screaming, screaming, baby,
for life, after it, around it,
screaming for life, *blow Bird!*

What is the meaning of music?
What is the meaning of war?
What is the meaning of oppression?
Blow Bird! Ripped up and down
into the interior of life, the pain,
Bird, the embraceable you,
how many brothers gone,
smacked out: blues and racism,
the hardest, longest penis
in the Mississippi urinal:
Blow Bird!

Taught more musicians, then forgot,
space loose, fouling the melodies,
the marching songs, the fine white
geese from the plantations,
syrup in this pork barrel,
Kansas City, the even teeth
of the mafia, the big band:
Blow Bird! Inside out Charlie's
guts, *Blow Bird!* get yourself killed.

In the first wave, the musicians,
out there, alone, in the first wave;
everywhere you went, Massey Hall,
Sweden, New Rochelle, *Birdland,*
nameless bird, Blue Note, Carnegie,
tuxedo junction, out of nowhere,
confirmation, confirmation, confirmation:
Bird Lives! Bird Lives! and you do:
Dead—

HISTORY AS SILENCE:
THE CORONER'S SONG

"Coroner," make out this yellow
sheet for an unknown name:
in the marketplace
the Mississippi
in plaid scotch print
rings under the eyes,
the brow eaten from the outside.

"There's a man goin' 'round
takin' names"—got yours,
though you carry no words
to identify what's torn
even the lining of your throat
in parts;

children, near the trolley,
on the cobblestones,
fight the rats with baseball
bats for exits and sewers;
and on your workbench
the ether of our scotch broth
tasting of rat poison:
"Coroner, sign your name!"

FIRST MEETING:
MID-WESTERN BLUES SONG: IOWA CITY, IOWA

Fine white blossoms on the water
dividing the campus;
we hook each other casting for color—
"talk to me baby, or they'll know
I'm a brother; let me get my knife"—
Ice broken in the humid light of the bank;
too rare a brother find to let it go—
we break into *Bird,*
geese with fingers and pointed shoes,
kicking, on the way out of town.

The shoeshine parlor is the black
stronghold, subcutaneous popping rags—
"look here, Jim, how'd y'all make
it in this motherfucker, huh?"

"Somebody's really tripping hard";
We live on the inner rings of blues
songs: history is a black woman anywhere,
in the kitchen, in the land.
Crisco, red apron, vaseline,
the humming cadence of grease
on the upbeat of heaven:
go on Gabriel with your badass self—

Thumbing the printed page
plates of painters shimmer:
memory plus photography
equals surface tension.
In stopaction TV,
lounge and lunchcounter,
these burnt faces peer.

Banked riverbanks
flow in nervous air,
the trees puff out
to us with our breathing,
shoe rags changed in their
blossoming, greasepaint
burned season by season.

IV

AERIAL VIEW: ST. LOUIS, MISSOURI:
HISTORY AS FLYPAPER

Up in the microbe sky
the flat caulked landscape
circles in the flittering
sunshine, brown stream,
brown belly of daylight,
pasture and harness,
river rising, moon all gone.

The tropical fish
flit as expressions,
photographs taken in height,
the land driven from conventions,
clots of trees, hair on each
face, lightning, thunder,
roaches marching in storm.

This is a child-care center,
the axed southern bench
initialed and scuffed
names and places
having killed black life
over again
into the banksides,
your scoured mucus
lining seared into song.

Eating the rat poison,
crystalized yogurt,
magnesium bombs,
the limbs of trees
blackened in kerosene,
flames, the swing band
of harmonicas, loaves
and pickles, the token
hands and feet,
the testicles;
lunch, a burnt crow
black, lye,
a bomb in the poplar
tree:
"Gail" the harpies sing
from the state of New York:
family tonnage,
the sick registers
of dry ice weeping
at the funeral:
swallowing rat poison,
in the dark,
an intestinal lynching,
swathed in the city museum.
The gateway to the west
is a half circle of blood
the back of rat
hurled, biting,
a furred chariot: *fly!*

Please Send Me Someone to Love

Zeus and memory
had nine daughters
precisely numbered
over the arts
and sciences:
a reducible number—
the square root of muse
is passion and no memory—
"History for us begins
with murder and enslavement
not with discovery."

Equipped with keyboards
circuits and recording
blight, logic, high
speeds, time and place,
these coded numbers:
reality: value: pattern.

"Apollo, sunburnt soulbrother,
true, learned paradigm,
what do your eyes see
in x-ray light at the horizon?"

"Apollo, I give you a prophecy:
what one doesn't remember
one can not forget.
Split on three beats
of music, this horizontal poem,
your dead black brother
steamrolls in the computer:
let the programs sing
to the sharks under water."

VI

HISTORY AS RAT POISON:
GAILGONE: GAIL'S SONG

Part I

Broken on the edge
of family memory
filtered and humid
I am the oldest
daughter, upper
New York State Scotch;
the rockbed feelings
turned in kitchen
pottery, African implements
tuned to the earth,
daughters at the hearth
as a druid eye,
and in the sky
African imagery upon me;
husband hurt so
his balm is the open
wound—his son—
St. Louis is hot linked
paintings, riverbed
music, death and minstrelsy.

Part II

Hair, black crow wings
picking you at the scalp;
eyes, dark, watching
nightwatch women, circling;
skin, diaphanous, peeling
shaled sunflower seeds,
nutriments in a flock.

Polished wooden apartment
in a homemade wall;
the nails hammer in
your wings
to the medicine pole:
Gail, gailgone, Gail:

You come back through veils
potted plant shrubbery
drugged into slower heartbeats,
violent antibreathstops
in our muted horns:
Gail, gailgone, Gail.

Witch or queen or sacrifice
your face hovers on canvas
and rock in this mural
we have painted you in:
Gail, gailgone, Gail—
rich in vapor, in song,
rich in wings, and in flight,
rich to the last breath:
Gail, gailgone, Gail.

VII

APOLLO VISION:
THE NATURE OF THE GRID

Blond, with a lyre,
his head a coin,
his eyes, money,
on the horizon,
an axis and this chariot
from the equator.

Of all knowledge,
of all reason,
numbers, sunrise,
sunset, time and place;
art, science,
meditation,
spirit, power,
contemplation:

no ritual; no dance;
no song; no spirit;
no man; no mode;
no cosmos; no color;
no birth; no death;
no myth; no totem;
no magic; no peace.

Potients and a map
to make up the muse:
"spirit, spirit on the wall,
give me paintbrush, vial and ball;
throw it into tapestry
substitute for memory"—

This grid, ideal,
intersecting squares,
system, thought,
western wall,
migrating phoenix,
death to all.

VIII

CHRISTIAN'S BOX SEAT: SO WHAT!

A boy and his body
in a box;
though his father's
arm is an ax;
father and son,
mother in the morgue,
and the country
wholly responsible.

Buried in the desert
are the true artifacts,
the slow Nile,
Osirus on congas,
a bitch named Isis
off into revenge.

Alcibiades,
you're breaking discipline
baby, it's hard
to keep on pushing
when you can't read
the signs or follow instructions.
Got a head like a sphinx-nigger—

You'll get a test
which you'll fail,
Christian;
even though you spell
backwards, and in rage,
pee down on your
signifying playmates,
you ain't gonna make it
in school,
less you learn
to clean up.

And in this man's
gallery, the loss of much
woman, and the images
coming on:
catch it,
on canvas, and on
the sink
'fore the water
runs dry.

Ancestors in African masks
beckon you to this fountain
where your father drinks,
and on the funeral pyre
your mother in this smoke
and a man running.

IX

HIGH MODES: VISION AS RITUAL:
CONFIRMATION

Black Man Go Back To The Old Country
Black Man Go Back To The Old Country
Black Man Go Back To The Old Country
Black Man Go Back To The Old Country

And you went back home for the images,
the brushwork packing the mud
into the human form; and the ritual:
Black Man Go Back To The Old Country.

We danced, the chocolate trees and samba
leaves wetting the paintbrush, and babies
came in whispering of one, oneness,
otherness, forming each man in his music,
one to one: and we touched, *contact-high,*
high modes, *contact-high,* and the images,
contact-high, man to man, came back.
Black Man Go Back To The Old Country.

The grooves turned in a human face,
Lady Day, blue and green, modally,
and we touched, *contact-high,* high modes:
Black Man Go Back To The Old Country.

Bird was a mode from the old country;
Bud Powell bowed in modality, blow Bud;
Louis Armstrong touched the old country,
and brought it back, around corners;
Miles is a mode; Coltrane is, power,
Black Man Go Back To The Old Country
Black Man Go Back To The Old Country
Black Man Go Back To The Old Country

And we go back to the well: Africa,
the first mode, and man, modally,
touched the land of the continent,
modality: we are one; a man is another
man's face, modality, in continuum,
from man, to man, *contact-high,* to man,
contact-high, to man, high modes, oneness,
contact-high, man to man, *contact-high:*

Black Man Go Back To The Old Country
Black Man Go Back To The Old Country
Black Man Go Back To The Old Country
Black Man Go Back To The Old Country

Michael S. Harper, a native of Brooklyn, is an associate
professor of English at Brown University. He is presently
(1970–71) a fellow in the Center for Advanced Study at the
University of Illinois. He has also taught at California State
College at Hayward, Reed College, Lewis and Clark College,
and Contra Costa College. He holds degrees from California
State College at Los Angeles and the University of Iowa.

His poems have appeared in many journals, including
*Poetry Northwest, Southern Review, Quarterly Review of
Literature, Negro Digest,* and *The Massachusetts Review.*
His first volume of poetry, *Dear John, Dear Coltrane,* was
published in 1970 by the University of Pittsburgh Press.